More Than Just a VEGETABLE GARDEN

Photos and Text by
Dwight Kuhn

Silver Press

To my daughter Michele.
Thanks for many hours weeding the garden.

Acknowledgments: Thanks go to my wife Kathy for her editorial help and her encouragement in the preparation of this book. I also wish to thank Neil Soderstrom for his valuable guidance and assistance from concept to final books in this MORE THAN JUST A ... series. Thanks too to this book's designer Andy Steigmeier and to Silver Press' Bonnie Brook and Leslie Bauman, who helped in shaping and designing the series.

Produced by Soderstrom Publishing Group Inc.
Book design by Andrew Steigmeier

Published by Silver Press, a division of
Silver Burdett Press, Inc.
Simon & Schuster, Inc.
Prentice Hall Bldg., Englewood Cliffs, NJ 07632

Library of Congress Cataloging-in-Publication Data

Kuhn, Dwight.
More than just a vegetable garden / text and photos by Dwight Kuhn. p.   cm.
Summary: Text and photos present life among the animals and plants in a vegetable garden. Also gives instructions for starting your own vegetable garden indoors.
1.Vegetable gardening—Juvenile literature. 2.Garden ecology—Juvenile literature. (1.Vegetable gardening. 2.Gardening. 3.Garden ecology. 4.Ecology.) I. Title
SB324.K84   1990   635—cd20   89-39504   CIP   AC
ISBN 0-671-69645-9   ISBN 0-671-69643-2 (lib. bdg.)

Printed in the United States of America

10 9 8 7 6 5 4 3 2 1

Vegetables grow from seeds like these. This growth seems
almost magic. Seeds sprout up. Leaves appear. Flowers
blossom. *Fruits* form with new seeds. This is the yearly
cycle in a plant's life. But there's more—much more—to life
in a vegetable garden.

This bean seed was soaked in water and then broken in half. Inside its protective shell, or seed coat, is a tiny baby plant with leaves. Around the baby plant are *seed leaves* full of food.

Bean seeds sprout when planted in warm, moist soil. First, a root grows downward. Then a stem lifts the seed out of the soil. Next the seed coat falls away. On the next page, you see *true leaves* at the top of the plant. They are creating food. You can also see round-shaped seed leaves attached to the stem. They are helping to feed the plant now but will soon fall away.

8 days

4

11 days

9 days

Vegetable plants can start from seeds. But some don't have to. For example, potato plants grow from rootlike stem parts called *tubers*. Each has little sprouts called eyes. If you plant a slice of potato with an eye in it, a new plant will grow.

Sprouting potato eyes

Strawberry plants can start from seeds too. But they also grow another way. Parent strawberry plants can send out stems called runners. At the end of each runner, a new plant begins to grow.

Star-nosed moles hunt for worms and insects by digging tunnels. Their digging can hurt plants because it pulls soil away from the roots.

Star-nosed mole

7

Earthworms are one of the garden's best friends. They eat their way through the soil, gobbling mouthfuls as they go.

The tunnels earthworms make let water and air reach plant roots. Heavy rains may fill the tunnels with water. Then the earthworms must come to the surface for air or else drown.

Earthworms use some of the soil for food. The rest passes out their tail end in funny-shaped clumps called castings. These have *nutrients* (NEW-tree-ents) that help plants grow.

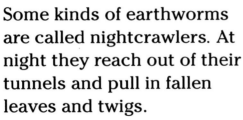

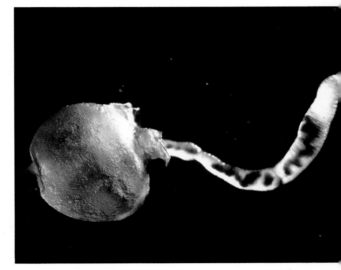

Some kinds of earthworms are called nightcrawlers. At night they reach out of their tunnels and pull in fallen leaves and twigs. Underground, leaves and twigs decay faster and so enrich the soil sooner.

Earthworms have a thick belt on their bodies. This belt produces an egg cocoon that the earthworm lays in the soil. Within a few weeks, little worms wiggle out. Can you guess what their first meal is? Soil of course.

Cocoon and baby worm

Young pumpkin plant

Like this young pumpkin, vegetable plants have roots, stems, and leaves. Roots anchor the plant in the soil. They also take in water and nutrients from the soil and store food. Stems carry water and nutrients from the roots to other parts of the plant.

Leaves make food for the plant. This process is called *photosynthesis* (fow-tow-SIN-thes-sis). Here energy from the sun helps green *chlorophyll* (KLOR-o-fill) in the leaves change water and air into food. This food travels through the stems to feed other parts of the plant.

People could not breathe without plants. That's because plants give off oxygen, a gas in the air that people need.

Pumpkin leaf

A weed is any plant you do not want in your garden.
Weeds steal water, nutrients, and growing space from
vegetables. So to help your vegetables, you should
pull out weeds. Sometimes young weeds look like
young vegetables. In this photo, the plant on the left is
a weed. The one on the right is a young corn plant.

Ladybug and aphid

Like weeds, some insects harm plants. Harmful insects feed on plants and spread plant diseases. But there are also helpful insects such as ladybug beetles and praying mantises. They eat many insects that harm vegetable plants. Ladybugs eat aphids and other tiny insects. Praying mantises often catch larger insects such as grasshoppers, flies, and beetles.

Beetle and praying mantis

Tomato flower

In the plant world, flowers have only one purpose. That's to make new seeds that will grow into new plants.

In a tomato flower, many male parts called *stamens* surround a single female part called a *pistil*. At the bottom of the pistil is a round swollen *ovary* that contains many eggs. The stamens make a dustlike *pollen*. If pollen lands on the pistil and joins with the eggs, seeds will form. Then the ovary will get bigger and become a fruit with seeds inside.

14

Seeds and fruits form after pollen reaches eggs inside
an ovary. How does pollen travel to the eggs?

For some plants, wind carries the pollen. Many other
plants need bees or other insects to carry pollen.

Insects like this bee visit flowers to drink sweet *nectar.*
Pollen sticks onto the insect. When the insect flies to
another flower, the pollen will rub off onto the pistil of this
new flower. This is called *pollination* (pol-i-NAY-shun).

Bee on pumpkin flower

Pumpkin flower

The young pumpkin plant below has already been pollinated (POL-i-nay-ted). The ovary is beginning to get bigger.

Pumpkin ovary

Fruits and other parts of garden plants often attract hungry creatures. Meadow mice may visit gardens day and night in search of food. You don't often see mice because they hide from people. A mother mouse may give birth to 8 or 9 litters of babies each year. Each litter may have 5 to 8 babies. So a mouse may have anywhere from 40 to 70 babies a year!

Slugs look like snails without the shell. A slug likes moist dark places because sunlight dries its skin quickly. A slug's life is in danger if its skin dries out. So slugs search for food only during the night or on rainy days. They like to eat tender leaves and fruits.

As plants grow, fruits and seeds are forming. Green seed pods have formed where pea flowers once were. Inside the pods are small peas to eat. Cucumber fruits are swollen ovaries with many seeds near the center. Corn kernels are really seeds.

Cucumber flower and fruits

Corn kernels

Broccoli

People eat many parts of vegetable plants, besides their seeds and fruits. When you eat celery, rhubarb, and asparagus, you are eating stems. When you eat lettuce, spinach, and cabbage, you are eating leaves.

Broccoli heads are flower buds. If you don't pick these buds, they will become flowers.

Be careful to wash vegetables before eating them. If you look closely here, you will see one good reason. Can you find the camouflaged tortoise beetle on this leaf? A tortoise is a turtle. Can you see why this beetle got its name?

Tortoise beetle

Many good-tasting vegetable parts grow underground.
Of these, radishes grow about the quickest of all.
These hot-tasting roots are ready to eat just 3 or 4
weeks after seed planting.

Radishes

Carrots   **Potatoes**

Carrots are roots too. Have you ever tried to pull up a carrot? Difficult, isn't it? Other tasty roots include beets and turnips.

Some vegetables that look like roots aren't roots at all. Potatoes are really stem parts that grow underground. These swollen stems store food for the rest of the plant.

Many insects harm garden plants. In the United States, the Colorado potato beetle eats leaves of potato plants. Without enough healthy leaves, potato plants die.

Green snake

Potato beetle larva, eggs, and adult

Potato beetle and American toad

In small gardens people pick off harmful insects. Creatures such as snakes and toads may help too. During a summer, a single large toad can eat up to 10,000 insects—including harmful beetles, caterpillars, and grasshoppers.

As the garden grows, more and more visitors arrive in search of food. Older box turtles like to eat vegetables and leaves. Younger box turtles prefer earthworms, slugs, snails, and insects. A box turtle may live for 100 years. It protects itself from bigger animals by drawing inside and closing its shell—tight as a box.

Tree swallows often fly over gardens. They swoop low to catch flying insects.

With frost on pumpkin leaves, this vegetable garden is near the end of its year's growth. By now, the other garden plants have died. Dead plants decay, forming a rich soil. From soil the plants began. To the soil they return. Over winter, the garden will rest.

If you have a chance, you might enjoy growing your own vegetables. And if you do, you might discover lots more than just a vegetable garden.

Starting Your Own Vegetable Garden

Starting Plants Indoors: In early spring, it's too cold outdoors for most plants. But you can start plants indoors and then transplant them outdoors when it's warmer. This lets you eat vegetables much sooner than if you wait. This also gives slow-growing plants such as tomatoes enough time to ripen before summer is over.

1 Here are some of the things you will need. Buy clean potting soil mix from a garden store. Don't use garden soil because it may have diseases, insects, or weed seeds. You could also buy plant containers called peat pots. Clean drinking cups or milk cartons work well too.

2 Use a nail to punch holes in the bottom of drinking cups and milk cartons. This lets water drain out. Peat pots, shown below, don't need holes because water can seep through them. Fill the containers with the potting soil mix.

3 Write the name of the plant on a small stake or Popsicle stick, using a pencil or waterproof ink. Push the stake in along the edge of the container. Place two seeds in each container. That way, if one seed doesn't sprout, the other probably will. Sprinkle just enough soil over the seeds to cover them. Pat the soil softly with your fingers.

4 Gently water. If the water uncovers the seeds, push the seeds back down into the soil. Water until the soil looks evenly moist.

5 Place the containers in a warm place. A tray underneath will catch any water that leaks through. When the soil begins to dry out, spray with a mister, or water with a small sprinkling can. Use just enough water to keep the soil moist. If the soil gets too dry, the sprouting plants may die.

6 When the plants have begun to sprout, put the containers in a warm sunny spot indoors. Remember to water them. If more than one seed sprouts, use a pair of scissors near the soil to cut off all but the healthiest sprout. Be gentle.

Getting the Garden Ready for Transplanting: When your seedlings are about 4 inches (10cm) tall, they are almost ready for transplanting. First they need to get used to being outside. Place the seedlings and containers outside for about a week in a partly shady place.

7 Choose a garden space that gets sun at least 6 hours a day. Turn the soil over with a shovel. Remove any plants already growing there. Try to make the soil loose and crumbly. Then rake it smooth and level.

8 Someone you know may have a *compost* pile. At its bottom will be a dark, soil-like layer called compost. This is rich in nutrients that plants need for growth. Compost comes from decayed plants and leaves. To learn how to make compost, see page 39 under "compost."

9 Transplant on a cloudy day or near evening. Otherwise, the sun may dry out your plants. Give them a thorough watering in their containers. Then use a ruler to measure the distance between planting holes. (The distance is on the seed package.) Make a planting hole bigger than the plant container. Pour water into each hole. Add a handful of compost if you have some.

10 If your containers are paper or plastic cartons, remove them. Do so by gently working the whole clump of soil out and placing it into the hole. Water thoroughly.

11 If your containers are peat pots, you can plant them directly into the hole. Make sure the top of the pot is below the soil surface. Peel the top edge away from the peat pot before planting. Cover the roots with soil. Water thoroughly.

Planting Seeds Directly into the Garden: First turn the soil over with a shovel. As you go, remove other plants. Try to make the soil as loose and crumbly as you can. Rake it smooth and level.

1 Place a stick into the soil to mark the end of the seed row. Put the seed package on top. Starting at this marker, make a furrow as shown. Your seed package will tell you how deep. Small seeds need only a shallow furrow. Keep the furrow straight.

2 Place the seeds in the furrow the correct distance apart. Follow directions on your seed package.

3 Cover the seeds with a fine layer of soil. Water gently. As the plants grow, sprinkle compost or other plant food on the soil near the stems.

4 After the plants sprout, carefully remove plants that will crowd the others as they grow. This is called thinning. Here you see lettuce sprouts and many harvested vegetables. Can you name them?

Glossary and Index

chlorophyll (KLOR-o-fill), page 10
Green coloring in plants. Leaf chlorophyll changes
water and air into plant food.

compost (KAHM-post), page 35
A soil-like mixture of decayed plants and leaves.
Compost is rich in nutrients that plants need to grow.
To make compost for the next year, place leaves and
old garden plants into a pile. Add dirt or
manure. Mix a few times during the summer.

fruit (FREWT), page 3
The part of any plant that contains seeds.

nectar (NEK-tar), page 16
A sweet liquid found in flowers. Bees gather nectar
and make it into honey.

nutrients (NEW-tree-ents), page 8
The important ingredients in food
that help plants and animals grow
and stay healthy.

ovary (OH-va-ree), page 14
The swollen part of the pistil.
The ovary contains eggs.

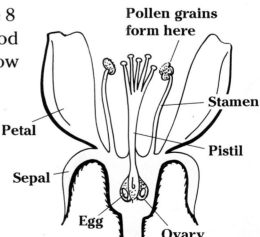

FLOWER PARTS

Pollen grains form here

Stamen

Pistil

Petal

Sepal

Egg

Ovary

(Continued)

39

photosynthesis (fow-tow-SIN-thes-sis), page 10
The making of food within plant leaves. When light shines on leaves, photosynthesis changes air and water into food.

pistil (PIS-tul), page 14
The female part of a flower.

pollen (POL-in), page 14
Dustlike grains on the tip of a stamen.

pollination (pol-i-NAY-shun), page 16
When pollen from a stamen lands on a pistil.

SPROUTING BEAN PLANT

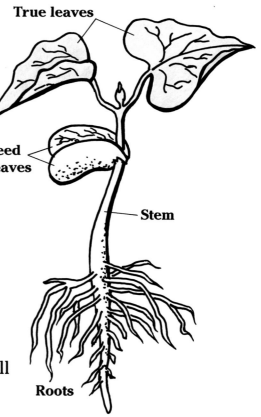

seed leaves (SEED-LEEVS), page 4
The first leaflike parts you see when a bean plant sprouts.

stamens (STAY-mens), page 14
Male parts of flowers that make dustlike grains called pollen.

tuber (TEW-bur), page 6
A short stem part that is usually underground. Some people mistake tubers for roots. A potato is a tuber.

true leaves (TREW-LEEVS), page 4
The leaves that appear after the seed leaves. They contain chlorophyll and make food for the plant.